The Book of Lurch

Virginia Larsen

with Jocelyn Pihlaja

Illustrated by Byron Johnson

DEDICATION

This book is dedicated to my brother Larry, whom I picture reclining on a cloud – barefoot, wiggling his toes, and smiling as Lurch glides about, trilling a joyful song.

CONTENTS

ACKNOWLEDGMENTS

I am indebted to my dear friend Jocelyn Pihlaja for her ideas, encouragement, and skillful editing (and for her clever chapter titles!) and to her husband Byron Johnson for capturing the essence of Lurch in his illustrations. Still, *The Book of Lurch* would have remained in my computer forever were it not for the technical skills of my beloved spouse Kirsten Lindbloom, who bridged the chasm between Amazon Createspace and me.

EARLY BIRD
Chapter 1

From the moment his beak pecked through the eggshell
that had protected him for three weeks of incubation,
Lurch was a marvel – a cockatiel so singular that even
now, 49 years later, he still, well, lurches across my mind's
eye periodically and makes me smile. He hatched, with
siblings, in a professor's home at the University of North
Dakota in 1967. His father belonged to the family of an
economics professor, and his mother belonged to the
family of a philosophy professor. He had august
credentials.

Although his siblings were physically normal, Lurch came
out of his shell with curled-up feet and a tail that, instead
of extending straight from his spine, pointed to the left.
My brother Larry, a friend of both professors, adopted
this physically handicapped birdlet and named him
"Lurch" for the way he propelled himself, heaving
forward, on a flat surface. Knowing his sister was both a
sucker for any animal and in need of companionship,

Larry built a Gothic-cathedral-looking cage out of dowels, put Lurch inside, and gave the whole works to me.

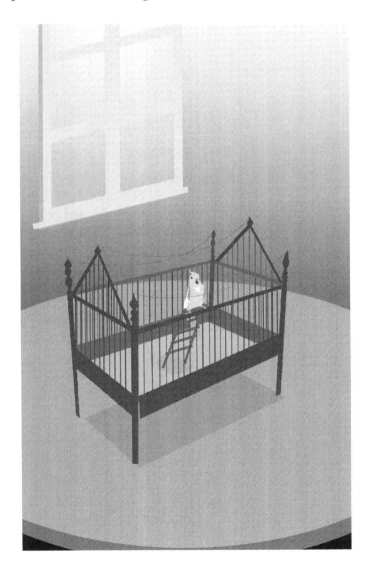

I was in my early 30's, recently divorced, teaching German and French at UND, and a pushover for any underdog, or in this case, underbird, whose chance at a fulfilling life would be enhanced by linking its destiny with mine. Larry and I owed our compassion for life's vulnerables to our mother, who died of a stroke at 37 when I was in second grade and he was just five. She had taught us that we could borrow but not keep non-dangerous wild creatures, like a three-foot bull snake or a glistening salamander, so as to learn about them before returning them to their original habitats.

There was no such caveat about adopting domestic creatures with special needs. And just as I believe some marriages are made in heaven, I believe, after sharing Lurch's life with him, certain matches between a human being and an animal are also made in heaven.

If my brother hadn't responded to some inner urging to select Lurch for me, this bird might have ended up sitting on the floor of a traditional birdcage for the whole of his existence. What a wasted life that would have been. Or he might have been picked on – or even pecked to death – by other cage-mates simply because he didn't measure up. Instead, he lived mostly cage-free, sang regularly at a nursing home, went to college occasionally, and interacted with all kinds of people face-to-beak.

I, too, profited from this match. I learned a lot about birds in general and how one bird specifically compensated for his inability to perch or to hop or to steer while flying. More lastingly, I learned that friendship can come from surprising places.

The moment I reached through the open top of Lurch's cathedral cage and stroked his crest marked the beginning of a 14-year relationship that left many indelible impressions on me. Because Lurch was so distinctive, so obstinately his own self, he also endures in the recollections of many people in North Dakota and Minnesota. Here I am, decades after his story ended, still smiling at how much *joie de vivre* was contained inside his delicate crooked frame and how compatible we were. Like any good match, we simultaneously doted upon one another while taking each other for granted.

BIRD'S EYE VIEW
Chapter 2

Lurch lived with me in a rental house in Grand Forks for several years while I taught at UND. I needed to take him with me whenever I went to visit my family in Bismarck, half-way across the state, because I couldn't bear the idea of his being alone for several days and sleeping uncovered. There was no one I wanted to impose upon to sit with him and sing to or with him for hours each day and tuck him in at night. Without another caretaker, he became my travel companion.

Of course, I could not transport his unwieldy Gothic dwelling. So how to take him along on this 500-mile road trip? Fortunately, one day as I was strolling down an alley, I spied a rather beat-up canary cage in someone's trash and knew treasure when I saw it. Spotting that cage was like finding gold I hadn't even thought to pan for. Excited, I dropped my briefcase onto the gravel, looked both ways to make sure I was alone, held my nose with my left hand, and plunged through some rotting tomatoes to retrieve the rather sorry configuration of bent wires. I shook a wilted lettuce leaf off its frame, tucked it under one arm and my briefcase under the other, and marched home, whereupon I introduced Lurch to his mobile digs. We were ready to roll.

A word about basic aviation. Lurch did not enjoy flying on his own. A bird's tail is the rudder, but the unusual angle of his meant that he could not steer in a straight line. Instead, he flew left, described a circle, then more or less crash-landed behind the starting point, making contact with a wall and fluttering to the floor – or, if no wall was present, hurtling earthward like a plane without engine power in a windstorm and then skidding on the runway in a flurry of wing feathers and shrieks. There was an advantage to his handicap, though, and it was that he didn't need to be caged, except for sleeping – and for traveling by car across the eastern half of North Dakota to Bismarck.

My parents and my four brothers were used to my bringing home strays, whether it was a student temporarily lost in life's shuffle, a quivering bunny whose mother had met a bad end in the teeth of a tractor-mower, or a one-eyed cat looking for a permanent address. Thus, Lurch would be just another house guest, hardly worth a second blink from those who knew me well.

The first time we traveled across North Dakota in my red VW, I placed the canary cage, with Lurch in it, on the floor in front of the passenger's seat. He was on the bottom of the cage since his limp toes did not allow him to perch on a bar. It was duskily dim down there, and boring, with only a black floor mat, black seat upholstery, a black passenger door, and the underside of the black dashboard to look at. He screeched in alarm when I took a corner too fast, causing him to slide into the wires of his cage. Repentant, I slowed down for every curve from that point on.

After about 50 miles, Lurch looked peaked. Tracking the lane lines with one eye, I used the other to peer down at my passenger. Once, I pulled over onto the shoulder to ask him if he was okay. To the extent a bird can whimper, Lurch did, but without a bird-sized dose of Dramamine in my purse, I had nothing to offer, so I pulled back onto the highway, and we continued driving.

Somewhere between Valley City and Jamestown, Lurch's crest flattened against his head, and his eyelids closed halfway. Suddenly his head began bobbing, and then he shook his head back and forth, spewing out little clumps of half-digested millet seeds stuck together with digestive juices. Some of the seeds adhered to his crest, others to his chest feathers, others to his back. My empathy was instantaneous, his sorry state reminding me of my two summers as a college girl waitressing on a pleasure steamer crossing the Great Lakes during which I vomited every time there was a storm, especially if it struck at mealtime. Lurch threw up on an interstate highway midway between the Atlantic and Pacific coasts, whereas I had vomited into every Great Lake. Clearly, we were soulmates.

We came upon a rest stop in a mile or so. After parking the VW, I lifted him out of his cage, a sorry little handful. We went inside where I held him up to the water fountain and turned on the water with my free hand. He ducked his head under the spout a couple of times and then drank a little before fluffing out his now-clean feathers. Looking up at me with one bright eye, he tweeted a robust note as if to say, "Okay. Better now. On with the show!"

I was amazed at his resilience and resolved then and there to find a better way for him to travel before we went another mile. As was my way, I prayed for an idea and got one two seconds later.

It would require a five-foot length of rope. I went up to the vehicles parked next to mine, knocked on the windows, and asked if anyone had some rope or twine. After I paid a truck driver a buck for some twine, he helped me tie the ends to the hooks above the backseat windows where traveling salesmen hung their shirts. My thought was that suspending Lurch's cage, with him in it, would give him the feeling of swaying in, say, a eucalyptus tree. I hoped to tap into a primal instinct buried somewhere in his genes.

With his cage thusly suspended, I set him inside. When we pulled back onto the highway, it swayed gently. I watched Lurch in the rear-view mirror as he climbed out of the suspended cage and worked his way laboriously to the top of it, using his beak for grasping and his feet for pushing. Once up top, he surveyed the plains of North Dakota, pumped his crest up and down a few times, and then burst into chirps and whistles as we passed a semi. From then on, he was an enthusiastic traveler. He seemed to love motion and daylight and, above all, the rush and roar of passing or being passed by a semi-truck, especially if it had colorful pictures of products painted on its side.

So enthusiastic a tourist was he, had we been able to drive to Hawaii, I'm sure he would have enjoyed a flowered shirt, a lei around his neck, and a pot of poi at which to peck.

BIRD BRAIN
Chapter 3

Craving companionship and, I suppose, a sense of control over his life, Lurch hated to see me leave the house. To him, my putting on clothing meant that I was getting ready to depart. He would rock from side to side and shriek even if I put on a sweater just to stay warm. And he hated the word "good-bye." Naturally, I had to leave the house regularly – how else to pay for my groceries and his birdseed? Even though I knew I would be back at a certain time, I could not make this clear to Lurch – despite explaining it in carefully articulated English before I walked out the door and got into my car. My last impression every time was of Lurch exhibiting the equivalent of a toddler's hysteria at being left behind.

His behavior left me conflicted. Why should I let a bird guilt me when I wasn't doing anything wrong? Who was the boss anyhow? For such a small being, he was a master manipulator. I wrestled with sympathy for his feelings and a desire to live a "normal" life.

My return always evoked enthusiastic trills and squawks. I wondered why Lurch reacted joyously when I called out "Hello!" but emitted anxiety shrieks when I said "Hi!" Eventually, I figured out that "hi" had the same vowel sound as the "bye" in "good-bye." Thereafter, I was careful to greet him with "Hello!" and not "Hi!" It occurred to me after a while that Lurch was training me, not vice versa. Our dynamic was not too different from babies training grown-ups to make goo-goo noises in high-pitched tones they would never use when communicating with each other.

I may have been the "grown-up," but in some ways, Lurch ruled the roost.

FINE FEATHERS MAKE FINE FRIENDS
Chapter 4

Lurch, of course, looked the same every day: gray body feathers tipped in white, yellow crest, and orange-feathered cheeks. What he saw when he looked at me varied every day, sometimes several times a day. He was unruffled by my appearance so long as my body was clothed and my face was uncovered – like a possessive boyfriend. I discovered this the first time I undressed in front of him.

When he saw me naked, he began hissing and bobbing back and forth. I suddenly felt as Adam and Eve must have felt in the Garden of Eden after eating the apple: hyper-conscious of nudity and full of shame. After that, I either draped a dish towel over his cage or undressed elsewhere. As I was starting to realize, Lurch set the rules in our house. I was in some cases a quick learner, but at other times I was slow to connect my behavior to certain reactions from him. Still, I was beginning to figure him out.

Two days before Lurch's first Halloween, I was invited to a costume party for UND faculty. I dressed as a cat and made myself an elegant black and gold mask of feline eyes and whiskers to fit over my eyeglasses. When Lurch saw me thus transformed, he became very upset, twitching and shrieking. It was as though the love of his life had suddenly disappeared, replaced by this strange creature. He seemed to know that cats were programmed to prey on birds, the creature he trusted had become the enemy. Poor Lurch. My costume had thrown him into existential crisis: if he couldn't trust his very own person to remain her true self, what *could* he count on?

As he communicated his joys and stresses to me, I began to see Lurch's life more clearly through his eyes. He was totally dependent on me for meeting his basic needs – for food, water, shelter, companionship and – this was my new insight – predictability. Is this not how it is with all of us? I had taken this for granted until Lurch's behaviors caused me to pause and consider. Predictability, dependability, reliability, consistency, habit, routine – there was nothing exciting or novel in those things, but, as Lurch demonstrated, we cannot grow into our best selves unless predictability can be taken for granted .

Lurch and I lived together for a dozen more Halloweens, but never again did he see me with my face covered. From the words I used to the way I looked, this six-ounce creature's wishes were so very often my command.

EATING LIKE A BIRD
Chapter 5

Lurch demonstrated that food tastes better when we eat with others, especially with people we like or love. He did not enjoy dining alone. Whenever I came home after a day of teaching, and we had greeted each other joyously, he nearly fell head-first into his dish of untouched food and began to eat as a caveman might have, making throaty noises of pleasure and scattering seed in every direction. The clacking of his beak was the equivalent of smacking one's lips, only I didn't notice, being too intent myself on raiding my own seed dish, i.e. the refrigerator.

Lurch liked it when I moistened my finger, dipped it in birdseed, and held it out for him to nibble. Even though he called the shots with me when it came to undressing, not wearing masks, and being careful about word choices and vowel sounds, he also relished a certain amount of dependency, where I was the giver and he the receiver –

like being fed by hand much as a small child enjoys being spoon-fed by a parent.

I usually let him sit in my left cupped hand while extending my right seed-coated index to him. He was very gentle and seemed to be tasting my finger or even caressing it with his tongue. In these moments, I felt a deepening connection to this physically helpless bird whose persona was becoming more complex by the day. I kept thinking of an infant, totally helpless and yet dictating its mother's responses. In truth, I can't say that I felt particularly maternal toward Lurch. I was more intrigued by the interplay between us and the subtle ways we seemed to anticipate what the other might do. If I put down my hand, palm up, for example, Lurch nearly always climbed onto it, eager to go wherever I might carry him. This trust that I would keep him safe increased my resolve to protect him from all possible danger without limiting his experience of the world outside of his canary cage.

BIRD WATCHER
Chapter 6

When Lurch was two, I taught a summer French course
at UND. During those warm months, I spent a lot of
time at my kitchen table working on lesson plans and
correcting assignments with my bare feet on the chair
across from me. Lurch enjoyed "swimming" around on
the table, nibbling the corner of papers and pooping here
and there. He had an uncanny knack for leaving a deposit
on the least promising French papers. The French word
for "poop" is "caca" – and Lurch mastered an articulation
of those two syllables, making them the only utterance of
his voluminous jabbering which was intelligible to my
linguist's ear.

One day during his tabletop investigations, he happened
to sidle up to the edge opposite me. Peering down, he
saw my bare toes. Evidently, he had no previous
recollection of seeing my bare feet during his aimless
wanderings across the several floors we had shared in our
life together. His gaze fixed on my toes, he uttered a

squawk of inquiry, sliding from low to high, as if to say "What? What is this?" Playfully, I wiggled my toes. He shrieked and, true to his name, lurched back. Then he swam over to the table's edge and looked again. I wiggled my toes again. He shrieked again. I wiggled them again. Then, fueled by a passion born in the depths of his avian soul and lungs, he began to sing. He warbled and crooned, and I waggled and joggled as he serenaded my feet.

Later that same day, Lurch was on the floor when I put on my shoes. He edged up and began to serenade my shoes. From that moment on, I could count on Lurch to perform arias in public. All I needed to do was stick my foot in front of his face. I called it his foot fetish, but his devotion to my peds was not warped. So pure was his adoration of feet and shoes, I would sooner call it a spiritual connection wherein his soul connected to my sole.

BIRD BATH
Chapter 7

All birds, wild and domestic, bathe from time to time if they have access to enough water. Lurch enjoyed splashing around in a shallow serving dish, dipping his head to wet his crest and flapping his wings in order to wash his "wing-pits." I offered him this opportunity to freshen up on weekends, when I wasn't in a hurry and he could splash all over the kitchen sink and wall and floor.

When he looked sufficiently bedraggled, I blotted him with a worn-out towel, and then he spent about half an hour preening. He had a little mirror and used it to talk to "that other bird," more than for grooming. His monologues had a tone of: "Hey there! You're some good-looking guy. Maybe not quite as handsome as I am, yet – oh pardon me, but you have a stray crest feather drooping to one side. Looks a bit damp. Here, I'll show you how to rub it against the underside of your wing to get all your bathwater out. There.

Now you look ready for whatever the day might bring! My person, Virginia, when she's not teaching, has no end of ideas and, except in winter, she likes to take me along in her car. We do lots of errands together. Sometimes I stay in the car, if she has brought my mobile home along. Sometimes I go into stores with her. She is always careful to hang onto my tail so I don't fall off her shoulder or fly away if something startles me. Well, I could go on and on, but I see that she is putting on her jacket, so that means she's leaving. If I screech loudly enough and don't stop, she will probably take me with her. I've got work to do. See you later, neighbor!"

I did take Lurch with me – from Grand Forks, on the northeastern edge of North Dakota, to Austin, on the southeastern border of Minnesota, to start a new teaching job at a community college. He adjusted beautifully because he had the three things that made him feel secure: me, his small cage for sleeping and traveling; and his most treasured companion: a leather glove named Esmeralda.

THE BIRDS AND THE BEES
Chapter 8

During the first several years of sharing our lives so freely with each other, I was the focus of Lurch's affection. Eventually, however, his eye wandered.

One day I was sorting winter wear and found a pigskin leather right-hand glove without a mate.

I laid it on the counter where Lurch was watching my activities. Possessed by passion, driven by a power beyond his control, as though he was identifying his paramour from a previous lifetime, he inched up to it, nudged it with his beak, and began to sing. I recognized the song; it was the same one he sang to my feet and shoes, sweeter than what he sang to the feet or shoes of anyone else. Lurch was in love. Examining the glove's nuances, considering the Quasimodo physique of its new lover, I named "her" Esmeralda.

Every evening from then on, at bedtime, I propped
Esmeralda against the outside of his canary cage, placed
Lurch gently inside, and covered them both with a dish
towel. In the dim and quiet intimacy that enveloped them
both, I often heard Lurch talking to her softly for a while
before I turned off the overhead light and went to bed.
Wafting through the wires of his cage, their pillow talk
was sweet.

A LITTLE BIRD TOLD THEM
Chapter 9

Because a community college is smaller and less formal than a university, and because I comprised the entire language department (German and French), I saw no reason why Lurch should not be my teaching assistant from time to time.

Lurch's debut in the classroom in Austin, Minnesota, contained the element of surprise, which cannot be replicated, of course. I wanted his introduction as my assistant to be as effective as possible. I would worry later about thinking up new elements of surprise to keep my language students motivated, engaged, and propelled further along the rocky road toward bilingualism. Lurch remained essentially monolingual all his life – or maybe non-lingual in that he never learned to repeat anything intelligible in English, though he certainly could distinguish between the vowel sounds in "hello" and "bye."

This is how it went the first day in both French and

German classes. The students in the German class seemed to understand more quickly what I was saying, perhaps because German is a more substantial language, in which things often sound like what they represent, whereas French is more mellifluent, sonorous, and musical but harder to visualize.

Scene - *French 101*:

I, hereafter referred to as Instructor, greet the class with a hearty "Bonjour, la classe!" to which they respond, in unison, "Bonjour, Madame!"

A chirp is heard from inside the instructor's lectern.

Instructor, feigning ignorance: "Qu'est-ce que c'est?" *What is it?*

Class, with puzzled looks: *???*

Instructor reaches inside lectern and withdraws a live bird, gray and white with orange cheeks and yellow crest feathers now rising and falling like hackles on a dog. Instructor places bird on left shoulder. Bird poops on left breast of Instructor's sweater. Instructor takes tissue from pocket and deftly removes *caca* from sweater, while repeating "Qu'est-ce que c'est?" and adding "C'est un oiseau," pointing to bird, and "C'est du caca," showing poop in tissue.

Instructor repeats question: "Qu'est-ce que c'est?" pointing to bird.

Class responds, more or less accurately: "C'est un oiseau." This sounds roughly like "Set ung wazoo." Good enough for a start.

Instructor exhibits product in tissue, asking "Qu'est-ce que c'est?"

The class looks blank.

One hand is raised: "Say caca!"

"C'est *du* caca," the instructor corrects approvingly.

The class repeats as one: "Say doo caca."

"Très bien!" says the instructor.

Instructor, looking at bird: "Comment s'appelle-t-il?" Pointing to bird: "Il s'appelle Monsieur Lurch." Looking at class and pointing to bird, "Comment s'appelle-t-il?"

Class looks blank. The same hand goes up: "Il s'appelle Monsieur Lurch."

"Très bien!" says the instructor. Lurch emits a shriek of delight and bobs his head up and down. The students are delighted and bob their heads up and down.

Scene - One hour later - *German 101*:

Instructor: "Guten Tag, meine Damen und Herren!"
Class: "Guten Tag, Fräulein Larsen!"

An excellently timed chirp comes from inside the lectern.

Instructor reaches in and extracts bird from lectern, placing bird on left shoulder.

Bird is gray and white with orange cheek feathers and a yellow crest.

Instructor, pointing to bird, asks: "Was ist das?"

Students raise eyebrows but do not answer.

Instructor: "Das ist ein Vogel. Was ist das?"

Students, in unison: "Das ist ein Vogel."

With unerring timing, bird poops on left breast of instructor's sweater. Instructor takes tissue from pocket and deftly removes *Ah-ah* from sweater, while repeating "Was ist das?" and adding "Das ist ein Vogel," pointing to bird, and "Das ist Ah-ah," showing poop in tissue.

Instructor, pointing to bird: "Was ist das?"

Half the class: "Das ist ein Vogel!"

The other half echoes: "Das ist ein Vogel!"

Instructor: "Sehr gut! Wie heißt der Vogel? Er heißt Herr

Lurch! Wie heißt er?"

Class: "Herr Lurch! Er heißt Herr Lurch!"

Instructor, showing poop in tissue a second time: "Und was ist das?"

Everyone, delighted at learning something practical: "Das ist Ah-ah!"

Instructor: "Wunderbar!"

Lurch bobs and weaves, obviously pleased with his success as a classroom teaching assistant. The class applauds. Herr Lurch, startled, flies off instructor's shoulder and into blackboard, then slides down to chalk tray, where he is scooped up by instructor.

No harm, no fowl.

BIRDS OF A FEATHER
Chapter 10

Once I borrowed an LP record of North American bird songs from the public library. Certain sounds made Lurch raise his crest, ruffle his feathers, and hiss as though the birds emitting those threatening noises might be in the next room. Other sounds brought out soft coos and chortles. A few elicited a whistle that ended like a question. As he listened, he was a study in total concentration: head cocked to one side, eyes bright but not seeing anything while he processed what was coming in through those ear holes camouflaged behind the orange feather circles on either side of his head. He was propped on his "elbows," or inverted knees, and the rest of him was as motionless as a statue.

Since cockatiels are indigenous to Australia, Lurch had only heard his "native tongue" in Grand Forks when he lived for a time with his parents and siblings. But who knows how many generations had passed since his first ancestors were captured by Dutch explorers and transported to the Netherlands before becoming popular pets throughout Europe and the United States?

What made him connect with certain bird calls of his adopted land as he listened to that LP record? Maybe it was something embedded in his genes – an evolution after several generations of cockatiels having heard American wild birds through open doors or windows of homes where his more immediate ancestors had lived. Maybe he was a natural polyglot, his brain instinctively translating the calls of American birds into Cockatiel. More than anything, I tend to believe it was the sound of human voices, especially mine, to which he responded from the heart.

THE BIRD HAS FLOWN
Chapter 11

One windy day, I was outside at a friend's house
inspecting the plants around her doorway. I probably
looked like a pirate since I had a bird on my shoulder.
Suddenly, a gust of wind caught us off guard, lofted
Lurch away from me, and deposited him onto the roof of
the two-story box-like house next door.

My hair stood on end, both from wind and fear, as I
shielded my eyes and peered towards the steep peak of
the neighbor's roof. I could see Lurch balancing
precariously on the ridge. Another gust, and he could be
wafted off the south slope and into, I hoped, my cupped
hands, or off the north slope and into a patch of
raspberry canes studded with thorns.

Agitated, I couldn't wait for his fate to be sealed. I ran
next door and rang the doorbell. Fortunately, the owner
was home. I asked if she had an extension ladder and, if
so, might I borrow it briefly. She had one, and I was

welcome to use it. A quick minute later, I put it in place, climbed up to the roof's edge – it was steep! – and spoke softly to Lurch, who swayed nervously from side to side on the ridge. Would he stay there and wait for me to inch my way up? This wasn't the first time I had prayed intensely on his behalf and, I suspected, it would not be the last. More willing to risk injury to myself than to him, I crawled up the roof's steep slope, heart in throat. Lurch sat very still, eyes fixed on me.

I talked gently and reassuringly to him on my way up and was relieved that he did not flap off into space. Eventually, we were reunited, nose to beak. He let me gather him into my hands, and we relaxed for a moment in the joy of reunion before beginning the precarious descent toward the ladder, which I easily climbed down using only one hand.

After that nerve-wracking rescue, life went on smoothly for a while – until a friend and I decided to visit Lake Louise State Park about 40 miles south of Austin, taking Lurch along. We were, all three of us, relaxing at the edge of a picnic area when a car back-fired, causing Lurch – always reactive to sudden noises – to flutter off in a panic and fly into some underbrush about 100 yards from the car. I searched and searched, calling his name, but did not hear even one panicky peep from him. It was growing dark.

My heart was in my throat as I imagined the dangers that might threaten him in the night. Would I choose to sleep in the car – with the windows down - in case he should call out to me? I didn't know what to do. What I did know was that I would not leave without him.

Then I noticed a spot of orange in some tall weeds. I stepped toward it and discovered that the spot of orange was Lurch's left cheek feathers. He was dangling from a weed stalk by his beak, like a rag hung out to dry. With his beak thusly engaged, he couldn't respond when I called his name: he was afraid of falling and couldn't see that he hung a mere foot from the ground.

Both episodes taught me not to be so cocky about having a cockatiel hooked loosely in the weave of the sweater on my shoulder. Only half facetiously, my friend suggested that I might consider a "Lurch leash" for future outings. But I decided to stick with the invisible tether that connected us: mutual devotion.

A RARE BIRD
Chapter 12

For a couple of years, I visited a resident at a local nursing home nearly every week and, except in winter, I usually took Lurch with me. When we entered, there were always a few old men and women sitting in the living room. Some of them seemed off in their own worlds, not reacting at all when spoken to. Yet Lurch had a way of communicating with their inner birds. All I had to do was place Lurch in an unresponsive lady's hand, take her other hand, and say, "Now pet him. See how he likes it when you stroke his head? His crest goes up and down."

Then I would take Lurch and put him on the floor next to the lady's feet. Immediately, he would begin to serenade her shoes. Somehow sensing that something special was happening in her otherwise bland day, the sweet lady would look at me and smile as though we were in on a secret. We were.

Lurch and I performed our routine for several years at the nursing home. He always "got a rise" out of somebody who rarely responded to external stimuli. What was it about him that broke through their isolation and touched a chord deeply buried in the insulation of dementia? It was something pure, spontaneous, childlike – an encounter without expectations, rules, or restrictions. Although the reaction he elicited in these chronically unresponsive residents had no clear explanation, I decided that Lurch had a ministry.

A BIRD IN MY BOSOM
Chapter 13

At one point, I took a year off from teaching at UND to work on a master's degree in German at a university in Marburg, Germany. During my absence, Lurch stayed with his mother and two other cockatiels, probably cousins, who lived in a large wire cage at the philosophy professor's home where Lurch had hatched. We were very sorry to leave each other. He shrieked, and I wept. From time to time, I was reassured by letters that he was faring well in his group-living situation although he received no personal attention and never left the large low wire cage atop a square table in a spare room.

After my two semesters in Marburg, I returned to Grand Forks and went directly to the home of the philosophy professor to reclaim my bird. At first, I couldn't identify Lurch because all four cockatiels were crowded around the food dish, and I couldn't see their feet or determine the direction of their tails. Tentatively, I reached through the little doorway while calling his name. I held my breath, hardly daring to hope he would recognize me, prepared for a reciprocal rejection after leaving him so abruptly the year before – though how could I have explained to him that I would eventually come back to him? My hand empty and waiting, I held my breath.

As soon as I said, "Hello, Lurch!" one of them looked up, chirped loudly and sidled over to my hand. Was it the way I said his name? My tone of voice? Whatever it was, I picked him up, cupped my left hand, and placed him in it, facing me. I began to stroke his crest with my right index finger. He looked up at me, bent his head forward so that I could better stroke his crest, and made little chortling noises in his throat. I had tears in my eyes; perhaps he would have, too, if birds could tear up. That moment was one of great clarity: I loved this bird. We were meant for each other.

As we resettled into our previous life in Grand Forks, the main challenges were reconnecting with certain people vital to my daily existence and moving back into the rental house which Lurch and I called home. During the first week, I needed to run a flock of errands. The problem was Lurch: he now had separation anxiety. The moment he saw me head for the door with car key in hand, he began to bob and weave and shriek. It fairly broke my heart since I could not explain the length of my next absence, whether 20 minutes or five hours . . . or a year, for all he knew. Unable to bear his distress, I ended up taking him with me as I made the rounds – to the dentist, to my office at the university, to the grocery store. So long as he was with me, Lurch was happy in his beat-up canary cage.

I even risked taking him along through the drive-through car wash since I didn't fancy parking him in his cage on the grass outside the filling station while I guided my car through the attack of roaring, rolling brushes and squirting, soapy water. I placed him in his cage on the passenger seat while I obeyed the signs to drive forward, back up a little, and then put the car in park and turn off the motor. At first his crest stood straight up, and he was too shocked to utter a sound as the whirring soapy flaps attacked the windshield and caused the little VW to shake. But then he looked at me quizzically, almost beseechingly, and I smiled, said his name, and told him we were okay, that everything was all right. He apparently believed me, for as long as he stared at me, he sat still and silent and seemed accepting of what I had unleashed, even if it didn't make any sense to him. As external mayhem rocked the vehicle, we sat inside, calmly, quietly, completely content. His trust in me had been re-established.

After a week or so, Lurch didn't raise a fuss when I left to teach my classes or go out with friends. We settled into an easy routine. He was always happy when colleagues came over and was glad to sing for their shoes – or their feet if they were wearing sandals that slipped off easily. Rarely did a guest raise a foot to the height of the table for this performance; I usually placed Lurch on the floor and let him "swim" among a variety of feet and shoes, provided everyone was aware of his vulnerability down there among such "hard soles." Even without a lampshade on his head, Lurch was the life of the party.

A BIRD IN THE HAND
Chapter 14

One evening, on a whim, I slid Esmeralda onto my right hand and deposited Lurch into her bosom.

I secured his right foot between my thumb and index finger and waited to see what would happen. He pinched my gloved index finger with his beak to steady himself while wiggling his nether parts over the palm. Then he released his hold and began huffing and puffing while he continued to rub his privates on my palm. Faster and faster, he wiggled and huffed. Suddenly, he tensed, and a shudder ran through his body. He stiffened for an instant, eyes closed. Relaxing, he opened his eyes, looked at Esmeralda, and began to sing to her, first with tender chirps, then trills, then full-throated declarations, his voice rising higher and higher until it broke, at which point he started over with lower, softer notes.

My companion Lurch? That disabled, quirky, malformed bird? He was quite a lover. When I lifted him off

Esmeralda and placed him in his cage, there was a small drop of liquid pearl on the heel of the palm. I propped Esmeralda in her usual place against the wires of his cage. Discreetly, wanting to afford him the privacy to which he was entitled, even though it had been my hand he'd just romanced, I averted my gaze.

From then on, I "serviced" Lurch about once a week, and eventually the novelty wore off for me. Then I took to doing what many wives do when sex becomes routine: I read a magazine or studied cracks in the ceiling. To my credit, however, I never pictured another cockatiel in my mind as he pursued his pleasure.

FREE AS A BIRD
Chapter 15

One spring weekend in his fourteenth year, Lurch seemed listless. On that particular Saturday, a day when I had a list of errands and chores to accomplish, he sat on the floor of his cage and did not want to come out. I felt torn between staying with him and denying that anything was amiss by going about my Saturday activities. There was nothing I could do to perk him up, so, enveloping myself in denial, I left the house. When I came home in the afternoon, he seemed no worse. It bothered me that he refused to eat, but I let that pass. Since he slept on the floor of his cage anyway, I merely parked Esmeralda in her usual spot, told him I loved him, covered them both with their dish towel, drank a gin martini – my prescription for all ills – and went to bed.

When I uncovered his cage the next morning, Lurch was on his side, lifeless. I was stunned. Was he dead? How could he be dead – his eyes were open! I stared and stared as tears welled up inside me with the intensity of Old

Faithful before eruption. A keening sound came from the depths of me, a noise I had never before emitted. Something inside me wrenched my innards, and then I retched, right onto the floor. Tears squirted from my eyes, and my nose ran copiously from both nostrils, past my gaping mouth and down my chin.

"Oh, Lurch, Lurch," I wailed, "I am so sorry. Please come back. Don't go. I don't want to live without you. We belong together, you and me and Esmeralda. I love you so. Oh, Lurch, my sweet friend, I know you are gone, and you can't come back – but I'm sure you're in heaven, flying with a tail that points straight back! Of course you're in a better place, one where you can land on a limb and perch there with strong toes curved just right for sitting in a heavenly tree. Awww, my dear Lurch, I will miss you so, but already I am happy for you in your new surroundings and in your new strong body. It's okay, little one. You are okay, and I will be okay. Yes, yes, yes: everything is okay." Having talked myself to a place of acceptance and peace, I stopped bibbering and cleaned up the floor.

That morning, I left Lurch lying in state for a couple of hours while I pondered where his earthly resting place should be and how he should be "laid out." He deserved to be farewelled with a certain amount of dignity and good taste, preferably with at least one mourner besides myself. I called a friend who had appreciated his uniqueness enough to warrant an invitation to his interment.

She came over, and we dug a 12"x12"x12" hole beside the back door. Gently, I wrapped Lurch in my favorite blue undershirt and slid him, thus enshrouded, inside a plastic bag. As my friend stood at respectful attention, I laid Lurch in the tiny grave and commended him to his Creator. Then it dawned on me: it was Pentecost Sunday.

As someone for whom religion had always provided great solace, I was overtaken by emotion: how fitting that Lurch should ascend on the anniversary of the Holy Spirit's descending on the first disciples! Would his brave spirit not rest upon me and accompany me for the remainder of my life in the form of memories and anecdotes I could share with others? I was convinced that it could – and it would. And it has.

Indeed, to this day and to my great comfort, all these decades later, whenever I envision Lurch in heaven, I imagine him as a Bird of Paradise, singing at the feet of God.

POST SCRIPTUM

I moved out of that rental house a few months after Lurch's demise, stored all my belongings, and went to Madagascar for a year of unpaid leave. When I returned in August of 1983, the house had been torn down, and the lot had been paved as parking space for the Catholic Parishes Credit Union next door. It was my intention then to order a bronze plaque with "Lurch Larsen Memorial Parking Lot" engraved on it; this I would place in the asphalt over his grave.

I never did order that plaque. But now, in these pages, instead of commemorating his death, I have tried to capture the uniqueness of his life and remind us all that, even between a human and an animal, love bridges the divide between life and what lies beyond.

NOTES TO THE ILLUSTRATOR,
FROM THE AUTHOR

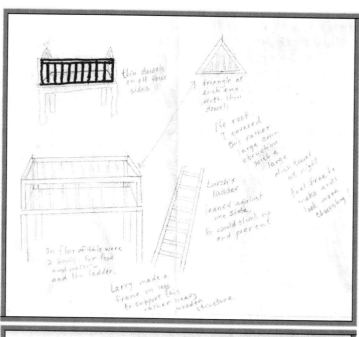

thin dowels on all four sides

triangle at each end with thin dowels

No roof - I covered this rather large construction with a large dish towel at night

Feel free to make ends look more cleverly

Lurch's ladder

leaned against one side, so he could climb up and peer out

On floor of this were 2 bowls, for food and water, and the ladder

Larry made a frame on legs to support this rather heavy wooden structure.

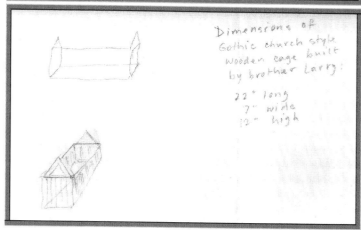

Dimensions of Gothic church style wooden cage built by brother Larry:

22" long
7" wide
12" high

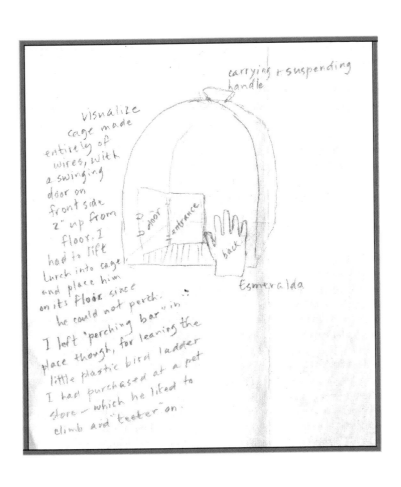

carrying + suspending handle

Visualize cage made entirely of wires, with a swinging door on front side 2" up from floor. I had to lift Lurch into cage and place him on its floor since he could not perch.

door

entrance

back

Esmeralda

I left "perching bar" in place though, for leaning the little plastic bird ladder I had purchased at a pet store — which he liked to climb and "teeter" on.

Made in the USA
Lexington, KY
03 July 2017